The Trap, Exit and Reward:
Setting Creation Free

I0200654

By Bob Mumford

LIFECHANGERS ®

P.O. Box 3709 ❖ Cookeville, TN 38502
931.520.3730 ❖ lc@lifechangers.org

PLUMBLINE

Published by:

LIFECHANGERS®
LIBRARY SERIES

P.O. Box 3709 | Cookeville, TN 38502
(800) 521-5676 | www.lifechangers.org

All Rights Reserved
ISBN 978-1-940054-01-8

© 2013 Lifechangers
All Rights Reserved
Printed in the United States of America

The Trap, Exit and Reward
Setting Creation Free

By Bob Mumford

The Trap, the Exit and the Reward Setting Creation Free

Contents

The Trap, the Exit and the Reward: Setting Creation Free

Our Father as Creator and Redeemer is restoring the Kingdom as His purpose and intent for the earth. This *Plumbline* is a proceeding word intended to help us discover our way out of cyclical, never-ending devotional Christianity (religion) and focus us on Father's Kingdom. Like salmon swimming upstream to deposit their eggs, the urgency is cosmic. I am speaking governmentally, not in ecclesial terminology. In no way am I neglecting or attacking the church, but the church is not the focus of this writing. We must center on the Kingdom. When Jesus preached the Kingdom He didn't say, "Believe on Me, I am going to die for you and be your Savior." He said something exceedingly different: "Repent, for the kingdom of heaven is at hand" (see Matt. 4:17).

Maturing in *Agape* is a cosmic event; it affects everything and everyone around us. One of our Kingdom presuppositions is that *Agape* is the absolute focus of and medium for Christ's presence and rule in the cosmos. Being perfect as Father is perfect (see Matt. 5:48) means growing up and developing Kingdom responses to inevitable situations that will occur. Paul explains this in Ephesians 5:1-2:

THEREFORE BE imitators of God [copy Him and follow His example], as well-beloved children [imitate their father]. And walk in Agape, [esteeming and delighting in one another] as Christ loved us and gave Himself up for us, a slain offering and sacrifice to God [for you, so that it became] a sweet fragrance (AMP).

Clearly stated, *imitating* God as a Father is a *governmental* mandate. *Eros* and darkness work on the same type of mandate:

You are of your father, the devil, and it is your will to practice the lusts and gratify the desires [which are characteristic] of your father. He was a murderer from the beginning and does not stand in the truth, because there is no truth in him. When he speaks a falsehood, he speaks what is natural to him, for he is a liar [himself] and the father of lies and of all that is false (John 8:44 AMP).

The Kingdom consists of the governing aspects of Father's own DNA (compassionate, gracious, slow to anger, merciful, truthful, faithful, and forgiving), which are being made incarnate in us as we mature in *Agape*! Defining the Kingdom in this light would mean *the cessation of internal conflict within our will and emotions.* To be free of internal conflict requires some emotional maturity.

EQ vs. IQ

> *Knowledge* [IQ] *puffs up, but love* [Agape, EQ] *edifies* (1 Corinthians 8:1 NKJV).

The biblical implications of intellectual quotient (IQ) and emotional quotient (EQ) are far-reaching. They identify the extent to which we have missed understanding that living according to Kingdom principles is Father's intended purpose. Daniel Goleman wrote a book called *Emotional Intelligence* skillfully explaining why EQ matters more than IQ. Emotional intelligence (EI or EQ) is the ability to identify, assess, and control our emotions. EQ is growing up emotionally. In the Greek, the word for maturity is *telios,* which means reaching the intended goal or mark.

Gnosis is the Greek word for intellectual knowledge, in the sense that, for example, we *know* it is sunny outside. I *know* that if I hit my thumb with a hammer it is going to hurt. *Epignosko* is more than intellectual knowledge; it means a strengthened form of knowing that becomes experiential, comprehensive, and internalized. Interpreting for you *what it is like* to hit my thumb with a hammer is *epignosko,* a strengthened form of knowledge. If I don't experience it, it is nearly impossible for me to tell you what the pain is like.

If you're left out of a group and you pout about it, you will probably be puffed up if you were let into the group. Can we see the emotional maturity in this statement? There is nothing more damaging than knowing your friends are all watching a football game and didn't invite you. It is an emotional issue, and it doesn't matter how old you are or what your IQ is. We still pout when we don't get what we want.

The only way we can become mature is by allowing *Agape* to bring us there. Nothing can deal with our emotions like *Agape*; it can take abuse and can cover human failure. There are times when poor behavior has to be confronted, but there are also times when it needs to be covered. Emotional maturity knows when to confront and when to cover. This challenges us to our core because the legalist in us wants to confront everything while the compromiser in us avoids all confrontation. Neither end of the spectrum is emotional maturity. It seems the church, including its leaders, is emotionally immature. We focus on being intellectual; very few pastors are teaching their people how to grow up emotionally. EQ, as compared to IQ, explains the complexity, competition, and multiplied failure of our present leadership. Father's wisdom is more than IQ and EQ; it is uncreated reality, which carries the label "*Agape* as God's nature."

Once we comprehend emotional maturity, we can better understand emotional *im*maturity. This includes road rage, jealousy, and competition. In my travels over the years I've observed famous men who were both intellectual giants and emotional children. I had a friend who was a very powerful leader in the Christian community. He came to our fairly large Ft. Lauderdale Bible class and said, "Bob, I'm just here to be with you. I don't want to be introduced." I believed what he said so I didn't introduce him. What do you think happened? He was offended and left the next day before we could even have breakfast.

Over the years I have had my emotions so beat up, expanded, trampled on, worked over, and challenged to the point that you'd think I'd be the "emotional giant" in the room. In desperation, I have cried, "Lord, if You don't let up, I'm going to die!" He said, "That's what I've been waiting for!"

The Seven Giants shown in this diagram consist of the inexorable rule of the ego. Each of the Seven Giants presents a distinct EQ issue including abject failure in

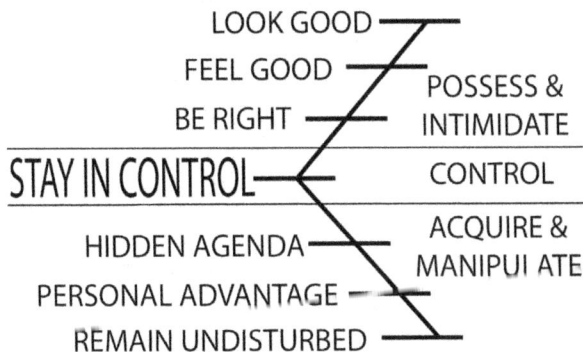

LOOK GOOD
FEEL GOOD
BE RIGHT   POSSESS & INTIMIDATE
STAY IN CONTROL   CONTROL
HIDDEN AGENDA   ACQUIRE & MANIPULATE
PERSONAL ADVANTAGE
REMAIN UNDISTURBED

the presence of brilliancy and reputation rather than facing an uncomfortable situation and accepting it with joy, which is evidence of EQ. IQ *knows* what to do but it has the *inability* to do it. There is a realistic, inexorable distinction between desire and ability that only those with EQ can discover. Consider the high burnout rates, suicide, and cynicism in psychologists, counselors, and ministers who focus only on IQ—it is not a pretty picture! Focusing only on IQ continues to propagate the *mirage* of wholeness but keeps us from the *reality* of wholeness.

EQ emerges out of maturity (*telios*) in *Agape*. Maturity is explained in 1 John 4:17, "In this [union and communion with Him] love is brought to completion *and* attains perfection with us…" (AMP). It is acting like our Father and walking in His DNA. If we *Agape* each other, we will express it in everything we do. EQ yields the boxer's advantage: "Give it and take it!" It is *inclusive* rather than exclusive. EQ allows our heart and soul to *precede* our mind and strength. The Kingdom is quintessentially irrevocable and inescapable *Agape*. It is relational at all levels and in all functions because it consists of relationship between God and me, me and myself, and me and you. When in conflict, EQ keeps us at the center of Father's love. IQ puffs up, but EQ builds up.

EQ is not only lost and absent in the Body of Christ but in our political and economic leadership as well. The Seven Giants release the climate of fear resulting in one-upping each other and hidden agendas of competition. Father's intention is that we live in *Agape* well-being, but when the climate changes to *Eros* or fear, we find a measurable and palpable loss of freedom and creativity. This loss can be identified by the minimizing of our Kingdom inheritance of righteousness, peace, and joy (see Rom. 14:17), the absence of which results in a works-based religion.

Years ago, to predict dangerous storms, we used the Early Warning System with radar. Pride is our own personal Early Warning System. We can feel our arrogance growing and we know that we are getting to a dangerous place when that self-sufficiency begins to rear its ugly head. As a precaution, each of us needs to better self-govern our own actions. We *can* anticipate when we are walking into a dangerous situation. At these moments we had better keep a close watch on our mouths and our actions. A sign of maturity (EQ and IQ) is when this Early Warning System is working. We may still make poor choices, but the fact that we are aware of them is a sign of improvement.

The *solitary* way to move toward EQ is by developing relational maturity with God as Father, with ourselves, and with the people placed within our sphere. The immaturity began in Genesis when Adam and Eve ate the forbidden fruit, ran and hid from God, then blamed others for their sin. *We* are a nation full of immature people—not them, but *us*. Our IQ only takes us so far. Our EQ is what takes us to the Father because it allows Him to work through our entire being to fill us with *Agape* so that we can become one with Him.

Emotionalism vs. Emotions

Our emotions are under attack. Skeptics call revival events like Brownsville and Airport Vineyard emotionalism, but they forget that we were created in the image of God, which includes our emotions. Galatians 5:22–23 makes it clear that emotions are the fruit of Father's Spirit:

> *22 But the fruit of the [Holy] Spirit [the work which His presence within accomplishes] is love, joy (gladness), peace, patience (an even temper, forbearance), kindness, goodness (benevolence), faithfulness, 23 Gentleness (meekness, humility), self-control (self-restraint, continence). Against such things there is no law [that can bring a charge]. (AMP)*

Emotions like feeling tender, angry, sad, or happy are Father living in us. But there is a difference between emotionalism and emotions. Emotionalism is relying on or placing too much value on emotion. It is shallow; it emerges but does not take root so it disappears and produces no fruit. Emotionalism is a by-product of emotional immaturity. It isn't bad or wrong—there is an emotional component to all of our responses, but in our immaturity we carry it into emotionalism.

EQ Helps Us Know the Father

IQ is what many already have, but it doesn't guarantee much or bring about the change we need. It is EQ that becomes the moving factor in marriages, businesses, churches, and societies. A friend of mine is a born again Christian and hired a man who is also a believer. The position required that he sign a five-year no competition agreement when he started. During the seventh month of his employment the man challenged the owner over an idea he thought should be implemented. The owner told him in a very gracious manner that he didn't want to use his idea. Instead of responding in a mature manner, he quit the job and went to work for the lead competitor the following week. That is a prime example of a fifty year-old who has never been told "No" and who is teeming and ready to explode with emotional immaturity.

Our response as children of the Father is to begin praying the prayer, "Lord, let me grow up. Build Your character in me and mature me in Your *Agape,* so I can reflect Your love back to You." Father wants us to be emotionally mature. He wants us to have EQ so that when we get a flat tire, we don't blame it on the devil or feel we are under attack. Living a life of emotional maturity means we are increasingly being conformed to the image of Christ. God is *Agape*, so the more we replicate *Agape*, the more intimacy we have with Him and others. Remember, *knowledge* makes arrogant and *Agape* builds up.

Society and Emotional Immaturity

Our intellectualism results in distance and superiority, and it hurts people. Even our hunger for God can become an *Eros* phenomenon. Often the skill set we require for someone with a teaching gift is IQ. But think of how many teachers you know who are black and white, hardline, and uncompromising. Often being a teacher means you are expected or required to become overly certain, stubborn, and often, inconsiderate—someone who would cut off heads in the name of truth!

Everything that *corrupts* society fits into the category of emotional immaturity. Racial bigotry, lack of respect for elders, stealing, lying, murdering are all result of the perpetrators either feeling entitled or nursing their offense. The whole creation is held in bondage of creating false impressions that lead to corruption. Some form or manifestation of *Eros* keeps creation in bondage.

The kids in juvenile halls are there because they lack EQ. They are physically 19 years old but emotionally they act like 9-year-olds, making poor choices that land them in the slammer. This is even more disturbing when a 54-year-old CEO running a multi-level corporation has an EQ of a 9-year-old! We see this with leaders all the time. They get the job on an IQ or equal equity basis but are seriously lacking in EQ. When dealing with others, we need to evaluate what level of emotional maturity we are dealing with. If we could adeptly ascertain this, we would then know how to respond to that person when conflict arises.

Consider the story of Dennis Kucinich, a member of the U.S. House of Representatives, who sued a Capitol Hill cafeteria for damages after a 2008 incident in which he claimed to have suffered a severe injury when he bit into a sandwich and broke a tooth on an olive pit. The tooth became infected, which led to three dental surgeries. The law suit, which had claimed $150,000 in punitive damages, was settled with the defendant agreeing to pay for the representative's costs. It is hard to believe that this was about the money. It seems that Kucinich was lacking EQ and primarily wanted to get even or to be right.

So, as Father's followers, how do we know when we are standing up for something that is unjust or we are nurturing an offense and lacking EQ? The answer is in the fruit. "You shall know them by their fruits" (Matt. 7:16). If this is our model, we are evaluating not projecting judgment. If someone decides to take their marbles and go home, look at the fruit of their actions. Are they acting in anger like a child? Or, are they responding to an unjust situation that they no longer want to participate in? The enemy seeks to provoke a good man to do a dumb thing so that it reverberates and injures on a cosmic level. We must learn how to get free from the trap of emotional immaturity.

A Story About the Trap

The trap and the exit is an important insight into living in freedom in Father's Kingdom. I want to take some excerpts from a paper entitled "Bringing Down Civilization" written by Derrick Jensen. My comments are in brackets.

> It IS possible to get out of a trap. However, in order to break out of a prison, one first must confess to being in a prison [that is Kingdom repentance]. *The trap is man's **emotional** structure, his **character** structure. There is little use in devising systems of thought about the nature of the trap if the only thing to do in order to get out of the trap is to know the trap and to find the exit* [that is the Kingdom]. *Everything else is utterly useless: Singing hymns about the suffering in the trap, as the enslaved Negro does; or making poems about the beauty of freedom outside of the trap, dreamed of within the trap; or promising a life outside of the trap after death, as Catholicism promises*

its congregations; or confessing a semper ignoramus as do the resigned philosophers; or building a philosophic system around the despair of life within the trap, as did Schopenhauer; or dreaming up a superman who would be so much different from the man in the trap, as Nietzsche did, until, trapped in a lunatic asylum, he wrote, finally, the full truth about himself—too late....

The first thing to do is to find the exit out of the trap [that is the Kingdom; Jesus came to set us free. It is not heaven, it is free].

The nature of the trap has no interest whatsoever beyond this one crucial point: WHERE IS THE EXIT OUT OF THE TRAP?

One can decorate a trap to make life more comfortable in it. This is done by the Michelangelos and the Shakespeares and the Goethes. One can invent makeshift contraptions to secure longer life in the trap. This is done by the great scientists and physicians, the Meyers and the Pasteurs and the Flemings. One can devise great art in healing broken bones when one falls into the trap.

The crucial point still is and remains: to find the exit out of the trap. WHERE IS THE EXIT INTO THE ENDLESS OPEN SPACE?

The exit remains hidden [one of the most fascinating philosophies]. *It is the greatest riddle of all* [that is the mystery of the Kingdom]. *The most ridiculous as well as tragic thing is this:*

THE EXIT IS CLEARLY VISIBLE TO ALL TRAPPED IN THE HOLE. YET NOBODY SEEMS TO SEE IT. EVERYBODY KNOWS WHERE THE EXIT IS, YET NOBODY SEEMS TO MAKE A MOVE TOWARD IT. MORE: WHOEVER MOVES TOWARD THE EXIT, OR WHOEVER POINTS TOWARD IT IS DECLARED CRAZY OR A CRIMINAL OR A SINNER TO BURN IN HELL.

It turns out that the trouble is not with the trap or even with finding the exit. The trouble is WITHIN THE TRAPPED ONES [emotional immaturity that expresses, "I want what I want when I want it"; me now].

All this is, seen from outside the trap, incomprehensible to a simple mind. It is even somehow insane. Why don't they see and move toward the clearly visible exit? As soon as they get close to the exit they start screaming and run away from it. As soon as anyone among

them tries to get out, they kill him. Only a
very few slip out of the trap in the dark night
when everybody is asleep.

Wilhelm Reich[1]

You don't need a lid to keep crabs in a bucket. As soon as a crab climbs to the top of the bucket, the others pull him back down. If you say you are looking for the exit, other people in the trap with you will want to stop you. Decorating the trap to look like something it's not and inventing makeshift contraptions that seem to give us freedom is how religion operates. Religion knows that if we really understood and experienced biblical freedom, we wouldn't need it anymore. We are all trying to find our way out of the trap, and one of the rubber crutches we cling to is religion. Religion makes beautiful statements about life after we are out of the trap but preaches that there are only two ways out—pray the prayer to accept Jesus and go to Heaven or participation in the rapture.

The Trap and the Exit

The trap is *Eros* or the Seven Giants with its thick borders that keep us trapped in corruption. The world we live in, which generally includes the Church, doesn't recognize the Seven Giants. Most people are unaware that there is a trap. Instead of recognizing these seven

[1]Jensen, Derrick (2006). *Endgame: The Problem of Civilization*, Vol. 1. Seven Stories Press, NY. P. 249-250.

as individual issues, we lump them into one word: *morality*. By doing this we never identify the fullness of the trap. Second Peter 2:19 says, "promising them freedom while they themselves are slaves of *corruption*; for by what a man is overcome, by this he is enslaved."

The exit is *Agape*. In this diagram, *Agape* does not have borders around it because it is freedom. We must be born again through the exclusive Eternal Seed of Jesus Christ because the seeds of escape are in His DNA. The trap and the exit have nothing to do with Heaven or hell. The Eternal Seed brought us the seven attributes of His DNA that have the power to bring us to emotional maturity. As Christ is formed within us we begin to grow up. We get out of the trap by growing up and ruling our emotions.

EXIT   TRAP

Agape: God's Seven DNA Freedom	Eros: Seven Giants Vanity/Futility/Corruption
1) Compassion	1) Look Good External view vs. internal reality
2) Graciousness	2) Feel Good Avoiding any pain
3) Slow to Anger	3) Be Right Know it all
4) Merciful	4) Stay in Control Deception
5) Truth	5) Hidden Agenda False unity
6) Faithfulness	6) Personal Advantage Working the system for me
7) Forgiveness	7) Remain Undisturbed My vision is the end goal
HUMAN AS GOD INTENDS ← EXIT	INHUMAN

We learned that the Greek word for perfect or mature is *telios* meaning to hit the mark. Sin is biblically defined as missing the mark. Emotional immaturity is also missing the mark. It is often more accurate and less damaging to label failure as emotional immaturity than sin. When we see our shortcomings as part of the maturing process, a beautiful story begins to unfold. Our responses to each other are a clear sign of our level of maturity.

Years ago my wife and I found a beautiful conch shell on the ocean floor and took it to our hotel room. You can tell if a conch is in the shell by the fact that the opening is shut. So Judith looked at it and said, "There is a conch in there!" I responded, "No, the conch is not in there." She said, "I saw him." I said, "No, you didn't see him. There is no conch in that shell." Can you tell where this is going? I got really intense and she followed suit. All of a sudden a large hermit crab comes out of the conch and walks across the table in the hotel room. I was right—there was no conch in the shell. Judith was right—there was an animal in the shell. What I couldn't understand at the time was how deeply emotional I felt about it. To an emotionally immature person, being right can take on great strength, power, and force! To an emotionally mature person, being right is not that important. What difference does it make? Our maturity really is a cosmic event—it effects God's creation on many levels—so growing up becomes a very serious issue for believers.

How do we go about growing up? Many believe it is by studying more. If IQ could make me grow up, I'd be a giant. If the number of books I own had anything to do with my spiritual maturity, I'd be larger than the Jolly Green Giant. Entire churches have split over someone sitting in the wrong pew. Each of us must recognize that we are in the trap so that we can get out and be free. In evangelical circles "freedom" is interpreted as licentiousness—getting out from under all the rules. In liberal circles, "freedom" is interpreted as exclusivism—our group wasn't satisfying enough for you!

People need to know that there is a prison or trap as well as an exit and freedom. Until we see this, it is impossible to be free. So many people are hung up on whether or not they are going to Heaven or hell, but that is not the issue although it eventuates to that. The exclusiveness of Christ is not about Heaven and hell. The exclusiveness is that only Christ is our exit, and we are unable get out of the trap without Him! This journey from the trap to exit is the essence of "Your kingdom come. Your will be done, on earth as it is in heaven" (Matt. 6:10). We have been inseminated with the Eternal Seed and are born from above. The seven aspects of the Seed are going to bring forth fruit after its kind—Father's kind. Carrot seeds will not work; we have to utilize the DNA in the Seed of Jesus Christ, the Son of God. Even with everything we know of Christ and His Word and His Spirit, it is still unbelievably difficult to get out of the trap. I think this is so because many of us were not taught Kingdom along our journey; we were taught Heaven and hell, but the Kingdom is not the same thing as going to Heaven. We don't know that we are not free or recognize that there is a trap, let alone how to get out of it because we don't understand the Kingdom. Christians have gone without a Kingdom mentality for a few hundred years! With our impregnation of *Agape*, Jesus opened the door to the Kingdom and "it is no longer I who live, but Christ lives in me" (Gal. 2:20). The maturity of *Agape* displaces our immaturity, so as we grow in maturity, we are being transformed into freedom. *There is no way out of the trap except Christ is formed in us!* We can be forgiven for our sins, but that is not the issue; the issue is our freedom.

Surrendering Freedom for Feelings

I asked the Lord how I would know when I was free. He said, "You'll know you are free when you stop talking to the other drivers." That broke my heart because in traffic I still find myself at least thinking, "Where'd you get your driver's license, at Pep Boys?" That means I'm not completely free yet. For others it may be when they quit talking to the "religious Christians" from a place of condemnation, superiority, and judgment. It's ironic that even in our attempts to become free we can become bound by religion! All day long events remind us of where we are at and that we are not there yet. If we are not maturing, we fool ourselves into thinking how spiritual we are. And remember, there is no condemnation in the failure. When we miss it and talk to other drivers we can laugh when we realize what we are doing because the recognition is a sign that at least we're growing up! We can feel the updraft of the Lord calling us into His presence when we recognize that first *we are in the trap* and secondly, *that we are surrendering our freedom for our feelings.*

In our misguided efforts we can use our freedom in an *Eros* manner. As followers of our Father, we understand that we have good days and bad days. At times our lives seem to just flow out of the seven attributes of God, and a day later we completely act out of the Seven Giants. We just need to *abide* (see John 15:4). Living in freedom and abiding in Christ means we can say, "Lord, You saw what I just did and how I reacted. I'm beginning to understand what happened, but I need some help to get through this autonomic response." That it is being in relationship with Him.

When we find the exit, we find freedom. The Apostle Paul says, "It was for freedom that Christ set us free; therefore keep standing firm and do not be subject again to a yoke of slavery" (Gal. 5:1). We are called to freedom. Paul saw God's people going back to Judaism and the works of the flesh and warned them that they did not know what they were doing. Evangelicalism is how we navigate in the trap. Our Christian gospel songs are often about life in the trap. In my experience, 95% of people in the trap, me included, don't even realize it is a trap because everyone else is in it navigating it and decorating it. I think of the movie *Beautiful Minds* where the main character found freedom because he quit talking to the voices in his head. They didn't leave; he just quit talking to them.

There are millions of people out there who have received *Agape* by faith but have never implemented it in their daily lives. So many of us believe we are already set free because we prayed the prayer of salvation in Jesus' name. And now we have 80 million saved people who say they are free, but how many would you guess are still emotionally immature and surrendering their freedom for their feelings? Unfortunately, we've created something that nearly approximates a Jesus cult. Adding another 25 million of the same kind and persuasion will not make much difference. We may not even know they are here.

We indulge our feelings whether it is to be right or to get pleasure or to gain something we want for ourselves. It is a shift to Kingdom thinking to begin to implement Father's *Agape* in our day-to-day lives. The larger Church so desperately needs to make this shift to a Kingdom lifestyle. In our evangelical world, we are accepted as long as we do not identify with one of the "Samaritans," i.e., — Obama-supporting, divorced, homosexuals. I remember seeing a bumper sticker in California that said "Nuke the gay whales."

Without knowing it, the Church lives by a two-edged statement: we say the prayer and have Jesus but we still boldly hold unbiblical exclusivism and demonstrate an increasingly pharisaical value system. Having Christ as Savior is not enough to bring us to maturity; we must apply *Agape* in our daily lives. That is Kingdom.

For me, when I see the traffic light turning from green to amber I know that the red stop light is coming, and I may be faced with dealing with my feelings. I am beginning to recognize where my feelings are going so that I can make the conscience decision to surrender my little "feeling trips" for true freedom and begin to mature in *Agape*. When someone's feelings are more important to them than their freedom, they are often and easily offended when they "feel" that they have been crossed. The problem is not so much that we have huge problems, but that we are *immature problem-solvers*. We have received the Father's DNA by faith but have failed to engage and implement it. When we give into an emotional reaction, there is always a pushback. When we give into our feelings, we injure, trample, and contaminate the world around us. It functions like a drug fix. Our maturity is a *cosmic* event. It isn't a matter of whether or not the Lord loves us; that is a given. The issue is if we do not mature, we do not become the instruments in His hand for which He has cultivated and created us. We receive the *Eros* payoff of the Seven Giants instead of the freedom of *Agape*. Which do you want to choose?

Know that in this life we will never be 100% free, but we want to be moving toward a 60% *Agape*/40% *Eros* mixture and then growing to 70%/30%. When we do this we are living in incremental freedom toward *telios*. When we live in pursuit of this freedom, every failure is an iterative experience. Maturing itself is iterative in nature. This means we seldom do anything right the first time. Like riding a bicycle, we usually goof it up the first time, but we will get another chance and figure it out by the second or third attempt. In order to mature, we must embrace the risks and challenges and walk this thing out.

I recently found myself in a situation with someone that got really ugly and complicated. As believers we needed to work it out. I began to realize that I was backing out of the relationship because I didn't love this person enough to put up with all the complications. Father's *Agape* in us is a strong and powerful phenomenon, but we are always given the choice of whether or not we want to go there. Jesus said, "I will never let you go. I love you with an intense love in spite of all your crazies." By allowing Father to work His *Agape* in me and through me I began to surrender my feelings and realized that His gentle course-corrections in the situation were redemptive and not punishment. C.S. Lewis says that Father forgives us for all of our inconsistencies but His nature does not allow Him to cease delivering us from them. *He will never let us go!*

Sin and Emotional Immaturity

I have watched people struggle and suffer in the trap. Jesus, in John 8:32 said, "You shall know the truth and the truth shall set you free." Do you remember the Jews' response? With a Roman soldier standing beside them they said, "We have never been in bondage to any man!" (vs. 33). We live in unbelievable denial. Kingdom repentance recognizes that we are not free but in bondage.

This helps us put sin in its place. What is pornography, homosexuality, lying, stealing, and cheating? It is all *emotional immaturity*. It is saying, "I want to stay in denial and pretend I am not in bondage or trapped by my sin." And if we don't recognize we are trapped, we won't be able to take the exit when we find it. We know a number of people who see the exit but don't know how to get through it. When most people see the exit, they run from it. Why? Fear and control are the major factors. If we realize we are in bondage, we may have to lose control.

People are so constitutionally wounded that they are almost paralyzed from walking out the trap door. The good news is that when we refuse to go there, the Lord has a "Ways and Means Committee" to help us head toward the exit. Once we see the exit we have to ask ourselves, "Do I want Jesus to be my Lord? If I do, am I willing to accept the cost?" This is literally following Jesus into the Kingdom, the true mystery of the Gospel. I would like to believe that if we took a really wounded person and walked them through this with great discipline, love, and care and explaining to them what freedom is, what the trap is, what the exit is, that most people would give it a good shot. I think that is what Jesus meant when He said the harlots and publicans will get there before you—those wounded most will desire freedom the most.

Jesus understood that the Pharisees would struggle with taking the exit. I've found that the few people I know who don't know anything about our religious system believe that freedom is possible. Unfortunately the Church can suffer from too much head knowledge (IQ) and think: Why should I try the exit when everything I have is in Jesus? Religion has convinced me that if Jesus covered my weaknesses and failures, then I don't have any problems. When we don't take the exit, we start compensating with what I call anti-depressants—drugs, materialism, pornography—anything that keeps us from noticing that we are in the trap. Instead of letting *Agape* do its work, we just go shopping! If our congregations and our church leaders are cognizant of the change, we must ask how it changes how pastors pastor and teachers teach. In this environment of freedom, the Seven Giants rule of control, intimidation, and manipulation will have to be met with an evaluation of emotional maturity in church leadership, including financial integrity.

Dearest Dave

I want to approach the trap from a different point of view. This is an actual letter given to me by a close friend who counseled this couple (the names have been changed). This story of Brenda and Dave is a Class A exhibit of the subtleties of the trap.

> *My Dearest Dave,*
>
> *In a few weeks we will be married. I love you with all my heart but wanted to write this letter to you to warn you about me and explain what I have discovered to be part of my nature. Because of my love for you and my desire to see our marriage work for all of our lives it is imperative I tell you about me. I wish it was not so but the reality is it is. I feel that if I explain this it will equip you to not give in to me.*
>
> *I know me and even when I don't want it to be so I find because it is such a part of my nature it happens sometimes without me being aware. Do not read this as me not loving you but instead because I love you I am wanting to prevent it from happening in any way so as to negatively affect our marriage.*
>
> *Dave I will fight you on so many levels it scares me. But it's true. I will compete and fight you for control and authority in the home. In the morning and through the night I will try*

and take over. I don't know why I do so but I know I do. I do it through manipulation, and out and out confrontation really whatever means available to me I use. I don't like that part of me and I pray for change in my heart but until I get deliverance please be aware of this in my life. I plead with you now as we prepare for a lifetime commitment to each other, do not let me win. Please don't give in to me and don't compromise in anyway. The thing I love about you so much is that you are strong and self-assured. Your leadership brings safety and security to me in a way I have never experienced before. So please never give in to me no matter how much I fight or kick. I need you to maintain your strength over me. I know at times it might feel easier to just let me have my way but I beg you never let this happen. The reason is I know something else about myself and that is if you ever give in I will lose respect for you. I tell you this in advance because I love you so much and want our marriage to be happy and strong forever. I know over time God will help me to change in these areas but till then please be strong and maintain your authority, leadership and mastery over me. I am the happiest woman in the world when you do so. It makes me feel safe and secure.

There is no one I would rather spend the rest of my life with than you. If you will take what I have shared with you to heart we will always have a strong, intimate and loving relationship. You may make a mistake every now and then and find yourself giving in. The minute you do, stop everything and put me back in my place. I love you and always will but I need to respect you as well. This ensures that I will always respect you as well.

I love, respect, and honor you and now I can only hope the information I have shared will help ensure that will never change. You are my man. You are my rock, my security and my safety. I honor you, respect you and believe in you. Most importantly I accept, receive and embrace your leadership in our home. And now I hope it never changes.

Your lover, partner, friend, and wife to be, Brenda

You can hear the confession and fear in Brenda's voice. Confession of who she is and fear of what she is capable of. She knows she must be mature, but then she speaks of emotional immaturity. She is in the trap and she knows it...but she can't find her way out. She wants to discover the escape but, true to form, seeks to shift the responsibility on Dave to get her out. I spoke with Brenda several months later, and she asked me to not ever mention this letter again. A few months after this conversation they were divorced.

In our present culture we have an increasing numbers of believers and non-believers who are in this not-so-mysterious place. We say to Jesus, "Please, don't let me go my own way." I know I've prayed that. I could have written this very same letter to Him. Maybe the reason their marriage ended is because Dave tried to stand in that gap. Dave probably said, "Sweetheart, I tried to stop you because this is what you asked me to do." It took four months for her to get to this place with him. She had to stay in control, but with Dave following through with what she asked, she could not. Dave couldn't stand in that gap, but Jesus can. He will plow our hardened hearts, break us, deal with our control issues, and do whatever He needs to do to bring us to maturity.

As we have learned, a seven-word definition of the Kingdom is *cessation of conflict in the human will.* Conflict in any relationship is designed to bring us to emotional maturity. Brenda was not ignorant of her issues; however, she did not know how to get out. She shifted blame from herself to her husband. Brenda's story touches all of us deeply, almost as much as someone dealing with alcohol or drug addictions because she could see pieces of her issues and was able to respond fairly maturely in words. In actions, she was not capable of taking the exit. Even her letter was manipulative. Her story makes it obvious that it is not just the world that is in the trap. The whole church is in the trap and the only way out of that trap, saved or unsaved, is by *Agape* being formed in us.

Freedom Is Cosmic

The loss of our personal freedom is more than personal, corporate, or denominational; it is *cosmic* and affects the Kingdom. The "entire creation waits eagerly for the revealing of the sons of God…in hope that the creation itself also will be set free from its slavery to corruption into the freedom of the glory of the children of God" (Rom. 8:19-21). The whole creation gains the possibility of being set free when we begin to live in *Agape*! In other words, the price of our own cosmic loss caused by the absence of EQ must be paid by creation itself.

I want to show you why we need to get out of the trap. Let's look at Romans 8:19-29:

> *For the anxious longing of the creation waits eagerly for the revealing of the sons of God. For the creation was subjected to **futility**, not willingly, but because of Him who subjected it, in hope that the creation itself also will be set free from its slavery to **corruption** into the freedom of the glory of the children of God. For we know that the whole creation groans and suffers the pains of childbirth together*

*until now. And not only this, but also we
ourselves, having the first fruits of the Spirit,
even we ourselves groan within ourselves,
waiting eagerly for our adoption as sons,
the redemption of our body. For in hope we
have been saved, but hope that is seen is not
hope; for who hopes for what he already sees?
But if we hope for what we do not see, with
perseverance we wait eagerly for it. In the
same way the Spirit also helps our weakness;
for we do not know how to pray as we should,
but the Spirit Himself intercedes for us with
groaning's too deep for words; and He who
searches the hearts knows what the mind of the
Spirit is, because He intercedes for the saints
according to the will of God. And we know
that God causes all things to work together
for good to those who love God, to those who
are called according to His purpose. For those
whom He foreknew, He also predestined to
become conformed to the image of His Son, so
that He would be the firstborn among many
brethren.*

I am not playing games with your head, but I am
after something that is as important as anything I
know. Because we are emotionally immature we have
taught that all sin falls into two categories: *futility* and
corruption. These hold the *whole creation* in bondage.

Futility and corruption are the trap. When the Seven Giants are exposed, we begin walking in the freedom God intended for us.

It is not hard to see that the whole world is *corrupted*—the church itself, the leadership, the elders, the prophetic gifts. Judith and I once walked into a church in Miami, and we were dressed well. As soon as a female pastor saw us, she jumped to the microphone and said, "Thou art like Oral Roberts." Judith looked at me and said, "I think she's looking for new members." The gifts are being *corrupted*. In Michigan I was at a meeting where there were three prayer lines: a $1000 prayer line, a $200 prayer line, and a $50 prayer line. In the $1000 prayer line, the prophecies were more specific. This is where the Dunn & Bradstreet report comes in handy. Remember Jesus saying, "You have made My Father's house a den or robbers"? The deception is almost total—nobody believes anybody, so the trust factor is destroyed. Our trust needs to be restored! Trust factors begin to emerge when the Father's DNA starts to function in us in relational ways.

The whole creation is held in bondage to *futility* and *corruption* waiting for the revealing of the sons of God. Our freedom is cosmic. Whether or not we cease speaking to the other drivers affects more than just our personal world. *Our freedom contributes to the freedom of the whole universe!* The whole creation is waiting for a people to take the exit and find freedom. Our New

Birth is not just about redemption; it is about bringing freedom to the world around us. Is there any question that this is the essence of futility and corruption? When we live this way, we corrupt the whole church. The curse began with Adam's *corrupted* DNA back in Genesis. Freedom is the reverse of Adam's corrupted DNA and the reconstituting of the human personality.

The intent of the Kingdom is the *reconstitution* as contrasted or compared to the idea of reconstruction of the human personality. Our New Birth is designed to create a new personality, a human living the way God intended in the original creation. We have a new constitution so instead of showing compassion to look good or offering grace because it feels good we respond as Christ would. If that kind of freedom permeates society, the entire creation *can* be set free.

This is not idealism nor some form of utopianism. This is what Paul meant when he said, "It is no longer I who live but Christ lives in me" (Gal. 2:20). We are not *repairing* the old man; we are *displacing* him with the person of Christ. To do this we are required to be conformed to His image. It is redemptive and one of the most freeing things we will ever experience. So when we start to run from the exit, we are now able to respond, "Oh, Lord Jesus, live in me! Help me live in freedom, not in competition. I want to do others good." This is the manifestation of Christ and His Kingdom that we've been waiting for.

In Ephesians 6:19–23 (AMP) Paul says,

19 And [pray] also for me, that [freedom of] utterance may be given me, that I may open my mouth to proclaim boldly the mystery of the good news (the Gospel), 20 For which I am an ambassador in a coupling chain [in prison. Pray] that I may declare it boldly and courageously, as I ought to do….23 Peace be to the brethren, and love joined with faith, from God the Father and the Lord Jesus Christ (the Messiah, the Anointed One).

Peace is the cessation of conflict in the human will. Peace in my marriage means that the conflict between the two wills has been broken and we're walking and flowing together because we are emotionally growing up. Our Father is asking us to grow up because creation is waiting for us to grow up. *Agape* means we are not permitted to fake it (see Rom. 12:9). It means our love for each other is required to be real and authentic. Almost everything in our world around us functions out of deception, false impressions, and miscommunication especially television ads, marketing, and politics. But we are called to love with an *incorruptible* love, allowing *Agape* to be brought to maturity. No longer are we to live in vanity, futility, and corruption.

All of creation waits for us to find our freedom but we have to be bold enough and mature enough to walk through the exit to freedom. If we find our freedom, we can then impart that freedom to others. In a domino effect *our failures injure others and their failures injure even more*, so the ramifications become extensive.

The world is sick of external rules and religion; they cannot and will not enable us mature. We are becoming nauseous from the written or unwritten rules that being a Christian implies: that we don't smoke, drink, curse, or see R-rated movies. We must get to a place where we truly want to live in freedom. This may mean that we have a glass of wine when we are with others who don't drink wine. I was at dinner with about 21 people, and everyone ordered iced tea until about the eighth person, who said, "I would like a glass of red wine." Everyone following her ordered a glass of wine. Her courage gave everyone else the freedom to order what they wanted. In the Christian world it can really get ridiculous as we all try to be like each other, fearing to step out and be free.

John 1:12 states, "But as many as received Him, to them He gave the right to become children of God, *even* to those who believe in His name." Christ *is the exit from the trap*. If we receive Him, we are welcomed into His family. We have offered people forgiveness—which is part of it—but seldom have we offered them an *exit*. We teach that Jesus' sacrifice offers forgiveness, yet we left out the urgent concept of personal freedom. Yet freedom is what creation is crying out for! As a result, we live half-frustrated and clawing at the walls because we know there is more but no one seems to have the courage to tell us what it is.

Motivation and Identity

Exercising our freedom may cost us. There is an expensive price for freedom, so don't think I'm saying it comes without cost. If we reread the Gospels we see Jesus repeatedly confronting religion because He would not and could not let those around Him determine His governing agenda. In order to grow up, we need two things: *motivation* and *identity*.

First of all, our motivation for character change has to be exceedingly strong. If we are commanded to grow up, we just get angry. But if we're encouraged and mentored into the process and necessity of growing up because we'll know God better and our family and the world around us will be better off, then we are motivated.

The second thing is *identity*. If we think we need to grow up just to be somebody that others need us to be, we will run. We understand that we'll never measure up to whom and what others want us to be. We want to grow up *because* we are Father's children, seeking to be and become Father-pleasers and potential ambassadors for His Kingdom! What I'm reaching for is the motivation to embrace God's work in our lives and the realization that growing up is for *cosmic* reasons. Both intimacy with the Father and release of creation are cosmic. I think of Paul's warning in Galatians that if we keep biting and devouring one another, we'll be destroyed by each other. That is strong motivation to want to grow up! We have to have something more than religion or we aren't going to make it.

Maturing Through Authentic Community

Father's Kingdom is totally relational. *Christ gives us life and the Church, in community, gives us a place to live that life.* If we don't provide a vehicle to get through this exit, we will just go from the right side to the left side, bouncing back and forth and getting nowhere. The goal is instructing not only the Church but uninformed nations about the freedom of *Agape,* and without a vehicle of transportation, we are just giving them another pretty painted picture without any practicality. The only way we can transition from the trap to the exit is supernatural through the Spirit of God, and the vehicle in which that happens is in context of vital, authentic community. Sometimes that community is simply your spouse, immediate family, or a friend. We rely on the Holy Spirit every day to speak to our hearts to guide us, and He does His work in us through the training ground of relationships so that we grow up and become free. Without the Holy Spirit who is our Helper, community is like having a vehicle with no fuel to power it. I'm continually amazed how the Lord guides and speaks to my wife, Judith, in phenomenal ways like that. Sometimes I'm almost envious of the simplicity with which she engages the Holy Spirit.

The Church has lost its Kingdom commission and therefore, for the most part, has failed to function as the boot camp or training ground it was initially intended to be. We can strain and groan, swear, and promise not to engage pornography or to avoid some other moral transgression, but without someone showing us a picture of maturation and walking alongside us in the struggle, we will remain occupied with straining and groaning, living in repeated forgiveness without hope of ever discovering the exit and knowing Kingdom freedom in this present life. The Lord allows us to struggle so that we can see our need for a Helper and community because there is a deception in unbroken success. If everything we do is a success we are living in Never Never Land. Failure is what forces us to engage with others and the Holy Spirit and reveals to us that we are not free.

If we will make the effort to see this, a pile of religious stuff will melt and we'll emerge in a lifestyle of communicating with one another and authentically walking together like we've never experienced before. The *cosmic* dimension of finding our freedom is highly motivating and absolutely necessary in our maturing process. We need to let this work in us because it is emotional maturity we're after not just intellectual growth. As we journey together in community, we will find what is real. So we need both the Holy Spirit and a body of believers to walk through the maturing process with us. Finding the exit is one thing, but emotionally and intellectually embracing the exit is another. The struggles before us are designed by Father to help us determine what is real and what is eternal. It is Father's gift!

Sovereignty vs. Providence

> *Who has saved us and called us with a holy calling, not according to our works, but **according to His own purpose** and grace which was granted us in Christ Jesus from all eternity* (2 Timothy 1:9).

There are only two ways that we are governed by the living God—sovereignty and providence. If we boil this down to four-letter words, sovereignty is *rule* and providence is *care*. His sovereignty is His inexorable will being done in the earth because He is King. His

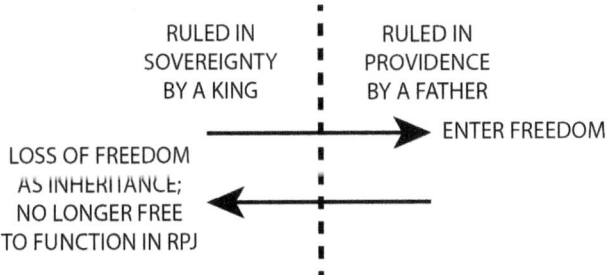

RULED IN
SOVEREIGNTY
BY A KING

RULED IN
PROVIDENCE
BY A FATHER

⟶ ENTER FREEDOM

LOSS OF FREEDOM
AS INHERITANCE;
NO LONGER FREE
TO FUNCTION IN RPJ

⟵

Providence is His Fatherly caring for us, guiding us in daily life. Father made a *sovereign* purchase of *all things* (see Rom. 8:28); consequently, He has the freedom to use *all things* in a *providential* manner.

Second Timothy 1:9 has been my life verse for many years because it confirms that He both saved us and called us into a holy calling not according to our works. Father has the freedom to choose anyone He wants, anytime He wants. Notice this Kingdom-focused phrase: "He saved us for His own purpose." He did not choose us so we can go to Heaven. Father's Kingdom calling is an invitation for us to *participate* in His sovereign purpose on earth. In contrast, evangelicalism, as presently practiced, offers repeated forgiveness so we can get to Heaven. Theologically, the acquired ability to repent and receive forgiveness from past sin is identified as post-baptismal sin. However, there is so much more! The hurting world needs Kingdom purpose and to understand the *cosmic* reasons for this purpose.

At age of 12, I had an unbelievable encounter with the sovereignty of God. While walking down the street with my sister, Diane, we heard a young couple in a store front playing a guitar and preaching the Gospel. They were with a small gathering of Nazarene students from Tribeca College in Nashville. Diane said to me, "Let's go in." We did and both of us gave our lives to the Lord. I was so impacted by the power of God that day that I felt like I was levitating off the floor.

Intense, unexpected persecution followed until I finally blasphemed God to get Him "off my back." For the next twelve years I walked in spiritual darkness. But interestingly, when I would go out drinking, alcohol, like a truth serum, would cause me to start witnessing to everyone in the bar. I was experiencing Father's providence. He promised to never leave us:

> *"For He [God] Himself has said, I will not in any way fail you nor give you up nor leave you without support. [I will] not, [I will] not, [I will] not in any degree leave you helpless nor forsake nor let [you] down (relax My hold on you)! [Assuredly not!]" (Hebrews 13:5 AMP).*

This is not a promise; it is a threat. Essentially He is saying, "You are Mine, and I will run you down and put My foot in your neck and bring you home if I need to. I will *not* leave you!" We are here because *He drew us here.* The sovereignty of God is His inexorable will, and His providence is that He will love us to the end, to the uttermost, *telios* (see John 13:1).

My wife, Judith, and I visited John Knox's house in Scotland once. In the foundation of the home were inscribed the words *God's Providence is Mine Inheritance.* I stood there stunned because in one sentence, he put both providence and inheritance together for me. We tend to see it as "I'm raising hell and living it up out there, but I can't escape God's government." Instead,

Father is calling us home. When we see him as our Father, we move from sovereignty or being *ruled* by a King and Creator to the security, identity, and belonging of living in God's providence. We have wrongly taught that the earth has been turned over to the devil, which biblically, is not accurate. Father claims, "All the earth is Mine!" (Ex. 19:5). When we tell Father we want *His providence to be our inheritance* we begin living in freedom, and our whole life is transformed. I want this regardless of the cost. Our providential relationship with Father provides *the escape* making the reality of following Jesus all the more impacting.

The phrase, "I bore you on eagles' wings and brought you to Myself" (Ex. 19:4) is *providential*. When a young eagle is ready to fly, the mother takes all the feathers out of the nest so the young eagle is no longer comfortable. Then she nudges him up to the edge of the nest and pushes him over so that the fall results in a struggle to use his wings, but she doesn't let him hit the ground. Instead, she flies under him and lifts him up to the nest again. She does this over and over until he is able to fly on his own.

C. S. Lewis in *The Problem of Pain* said, "Love may forgive all infirmities and love still in spite of them: but Love cannot cease to will their removal." God's love is unconditional, and He has a relentless, inexorable, commitment to our development and growth. He intends to crowd us to the exit. He is going to providentially move us where we need to go because His love forgives us all our mess-ups, but it is His unending determination that will cleanse us from them. The Seven Giants must die. C.S. Lewis saw this, but in his caution of being identified as a heretic, he slipped it in between the lines. We've all read his works and love his writings, yet he was free enough to smoke a pipe and drink whiskey. He knew the providence of God and how Father responded.

Jesus offers forgiveness but we've semantically raped the word "saved" because we leave out the second-half of His offer. *The concept of born again has essentially lost its meaning.* I encountered the Lord for the second time at age 24 when I was a medic in the Navy. I was home on leave and again my sister, Diane, invited me to a church service. Just to make her happy I went, and the very power of God came over my person. No one invited me forward, I just got up out of my chair and walked to the front and knelt down. I heard a young woman two rows back on my right grab hold of the pew in front of her and start an intercessory groan, "Oh God! Oh God!" Every time she voiced that painful cry, agony and heaviness were incrementally being lifted from me. The third time she groaned I turned around to help her because as a medic I thought maybe she was giving birth, but she was just interceding for me. In Navy uniform I stood up and said, "Ok, I'm free" and everyone clapped. The first thing I noticed was that I couldn't speak. I didn't have any adjectives to describe things. All my foul-mouth language suddenly stopped.

The second thing I noticed was that my desire for cigarettes was gone. I stood there not fully understanding what had happened but enjoying it.

If I would have lost my life when I was still seeking to avoid God and His purpose, His redemptive gift would have guaranteed my place in Heaven. Heaven is a destiny not a goal of life. *Providentially* our circumstances get crazy, but *sovereignly* we know who we are and where we are going to go. We have represented God as a judge in a court room when He is actually a Father with His family. The concept of Kingdom seeks to restore God's ownership in the earth.

We get trapped and unable to progress in our life in the Holy Spirit because of the limited understanding that our New Birth is all about being forgiven for our sins—but there is more! The prodigal and the elder brother are a good example. The prodigal comes home after partying away his inheritance and is forgiven. He's given a ring, a robe, and a pair of sandals. The ring is the restoration of his authority. The robe or cloak is the restoration of his righteousness. The sandals signify he is separated from the world. And the elder brother was *furious*. He said, "Look! For so many years I have been serving you and I have never neglected a command of yours; and *yet* you have never given me …!" (see Luke 15:29). The elder brother was a *foundationalist*. He failed to grasp that everything the Father had was already his. The prodigal came home as a *post-foundationalist*, realizing that he was not worthy. The sovereignty of God rules over the elder brother, and his father's providential appeal fell upon religiously deaf ears.

Jesus died for us so we could be forgiven and model our *providential* relationship with the Father. His declared and eternal purpose was to please His Father. Jesus did not come to die; He came to do the will of His Father, which included dying. This makes His sacrifice very real and personal. The death on the cross was an important part of His obedience, as martyrdom would be for you or me. The Father and our providential relationship with Him is the exit. This is what is happening in the book of John. The Apostle John seeks to take us by the hand and lead us through all the religious hallways until we reach the Father. We see this in Peter's escape route, too. It begins with faith and ends with *Agape*.

Peter's Exit from the Trap

Exiting from the trap requires a shaking of our foundations. When Jesus asked Peter if he loved Him, Peter's response was essentially, Lord, I know You intellectually (IQ) but not experientially (EQ). As Christians it is easy to just breeze by events that are designed to alter our very foundations. Peter's reformational experience in Acts 10 is a good example. When he had the vision of the sheet coming down and being told to eat unclean meats, he was beginning to understand that all the rules were being changed! Peter had never eaten any creeping thing; his foundation was certitude. *Then God said that what you held as holy before is no longer holy.* What makes something holy or unholy? Our Father's pleasure or displeasure! So when Father says something is not holy anymore, we should not engage in that any longer. The Lord patiently encountered Peter three times before his presuppositions could be changed. Then He sent him to Cornelius, a Gentile, with whom he could never have fellowshipped before. This experience showed him that *he was trapped* and looking for the exit, but he hadn't quite found it because when he got to Cornelius' house, he began by stating his prejudice that "God is no respecter of persons" (Acts 10:34)! Certitude may get you to Heaven, but it does not have the ability to provide you a Kingdom inheritance. Father tells us that "He who follows Me will not be walking in the dark, but will have the Light which is Life (John 8:12 AMP).

The other night I woke around 2:00 a.m. and I heard the Lord say to me in a most gentle, Fatherly voice, "Why don't you let the Apostle Peter walk you through the trap, the escape, and the reward?" Like Paul, Peter had his foundation shaken. He was mouthy and demanding and denied the Lord on three different occasions. Then Jesus restored him, and he was a completely different person—fully transformed. He went on to write some of the most important works in the New Testament. So, at the Lord's prompting, let's allow Peter to show us the exit from the trap. There are six steps in 2 Peter 1 that clearly outline the exit and how we can find our freedom.

1. Receiving the righteousness of God (2 Peter 1:1-2).

> *¹Simon Peter, a bond-servant and apostle of Jesus Christ, to those who have received a faith of the same kind as ours, **by the righteousness of our God and Savior, Jesus Christ**. ²Grace and **peace** be multiplied to you in the **knowledge** of God and of Jesus our Lord.*

Peter considered himself a bond-servant, the lowliest servant in the house, yet he received the righteousness of God by the incarnation and the DNA of the Eternal Seed. Peace, as I mentioned, is the cessation of conflict in the human will and is an evidence of the Kingdom. In Greek the knowledge of God is *epignosis*, a strengthened form of knowing that is not only IQ but EQ: as in I know you, the person. Peter was saying that spiritual knowledge acts as a workable road map enabling us to take the exit and enter that Kingdom sphere defined as righteousness, peace, and joy (see Rom. 14:17).

2. Allowing "all things" to bring us life (2 Peter 1:3).

*³seeing that His **divine power** has granted to us **everything** pertaining to life and godliness through the **true knowledge** of Him who called us by His **own glory** and excellence.*

His divine power intervened on our behalf through the insemination of the Eternal Seed/DNA giving us life and godliness so that we *can* find the exit and conduct ourselves the way Father wants us to conduct ourselves. Divine power is the Greek word *theios* and power is the Greek word *dynamis.* Remember this phrase because in a moment we're going to talk about the divine nature. We don't create it; it is His gift to us as we embrace His DNA—His own nature.

The phrase "*granted to us everything*" in Greek means "all things" and is also used in Romans 8:28, "And we know that God causes *all things* to work together for good to those who love God, to those who are called according to His purpose." God uses all things to make us human as God intended, conforming us to the image of Jesus Christ. He has chosen to give Himself to us through a strengthened form of knowledge.

The word "own" in the Greek is *idios* meaning *my very own* or a characteristic by which we can identify Him. This is where we get the word idiosyncrasies. We begin to mature through the strengthened knowledge (Greek *epignosis*) of Him who has called us to His own glory—His virtue or character. Peter is interpreting the incarnation for us. We can know the Father with this kind of spiritual knowledge because He has called us to His own glory and virtue and to be like Him. It is not something we manufacture but something He has provided for us.

3. Cultivating the promise of an exit (2 Peter 1:4).

> *⁴For by these He has granted to us His **precious and magnificent promises**, so that by them you may become **partakers** of the divine nature, having **escaped** the corruption that is in the world by **lust**.*

Note the phrase "*precious and magnificent promises.*" This is the clearest understanding of faith and *Agape* that I have ever seen. A few years ago the Lord said, "I am going to teach you faith and *Agape*." The only way to learn faith is to walk out the promises. When the promises have been fulfilled in our lives, they speak loudly of Father's providence. By these promises we become partakers, which in Greek is *koinonia*. This is Father sharing His DNA with us and our sharing of our lives with others in true community. Scripture is full of promises about the Seed, which is Father's DNA, and we receive them by faith. Once His DNA is in us, we allow it to become operative by faith and by hearing what the Lord says in His Word. One Scripture that impacted my life is, "He who follows Me will not walk in darkness, but will have the Light of life" (John 8:12).

God's Word is full of promises that are particularly ours, and we need the skill to protect the promises we have received.

With the foundation of verses 1 through 4, Peter then shows us that there is an exit: "*having escaped corruption that is in the world by lust.*" The Greek word for lust is *epithumia* (Strong's #1939), translated craving leading to *corruption*. We can, as astounding as it sounds, escape the entire humanly-created reality of the culture or world system that is based on deception, lust, and corruption. *Living in the Kingdom means we can walk out of corruption into freedom.* The means to this freedom is based on the promises, which give us the clearest picture of faith expressing itself through love.

4. Growing up and taking the exit (2 Peter 1:5-7).

> *⁵Now for this very reason also, applying all diligence, in your faith supply moral excellence, and in your moral excellence, knowledge, ⁶and in your knowledge, self-control, and in your self-control, perseverance, and in your perseverance, godliness, ⁷and in your godliness, brotherly kindness, and in your brotherly kindness, love.*

We are to *add to our faith*, which is the key to these promises. Peter shows us that taking the exit for the purpose of escaping corruption involves a maturation process. You can see the *iterative* nature of each of these: diligence, moral excellence, knowledge, self-control, perseverance, godliness, brotherly kindness, love. As we mature, an entrance will be given us into a life in the Kingdom by virtue of these promises being made alive in us producing righteousness and godliness.

Verse 6 says, *"perseverance (patience)"* The Greek word is *hupomone,* which means to be left standing up after everyone else has fallen. The servant of the Lord must be patient. Think how many times we've wanted to quit, but we don't quit. Godliness is the end result of the DNA formed in us 30/60/100.

Verse 7 states, *"and in your godliness, brotherly kindness, and in your brotherly kindness, love."* Colossians 3:12-15 is the same list of DNA again: "… put on tender mercies, kindness, humility, meekness, longsuffering *(hupomone* again); bearing with one another, and forgiving one another… put on love…." We start with *Agape* and we end with *Agape*.

5. Bearing fruit (2 Peter 1:8-9).

> *8For if these qualities are yours and are increasing, they render you neither useless nor unfruitful in the true knowledge of our Lord Jesus Christ. 9 For he who lacks these qualities is blind or short-sighted, having forgotten his purification from his former sins.*

These fruits measure everything. None of the fruits of the Holy Spirit can be imitated. If you measure everything by fruit not words, the results become a lot more real. Becoming barren or unfruitful may not seem to matter as long as we are guaranteed the repeated forgiveness of present day Christianity. I pray that our eyes can be opened to see this issue. If we possess these qualities in increasing measure they will keep us from being ineffective and unproductive in our knowledge of the Lord Jesus Christ.

We may be ignorant or forgetful that it is possible to be under the shelter of His redeeming act, so we remain blind and unfruitful. That is why another 25 million believers added to our churches would not make any significant difference. We are redeemed but we are blind and can't see what the issues are.

6. Displacing the Seven Giants with Christ's DNA (2 Peter 1:10).

> *10 Therefore, brethren, be all the more diligent to make certain about His calling and choosing you; for as long as you practice these things, you will never stumble;*

The Message says, *"Don't put it off; do it now. Do this, and you'll have your life on a firm footing."* The Greek word for "diligent" is *spoudasate,* which means to be zealous, active, and concerned about your calling and election. Peter knew that the internal Kingdom makes us unshakable. He was hammering this idea because he had been through the worst fall any man could experience when he betrayed Jesus and wanted to prevent us from falling in a similar manner. When his Master looked at him, it broke his heart. If he had the courage, he may even have tried to committed suicide like Judas. We must have the courage to look at all of this through that whole evangelical lens.

I wrestled with 2 Peter 1 for many years, especially the phrase "be all the more diligent" because it always sounded like we'd better get busy working harder. Getting out of the trap is not about doing good works; it is about *displacement*. Like inserting a wooden object into a full glass of water, Father seeks to displace our anger with His compassion. He displaces our hardness of heart with His mercy and compassion. He displaces our untruth with His truth. If we allow this displacement process to function, we will walk out of the trap into the freedom of the eternal, unshakable Kingdom. This is, as well, what is implied when we say "conformed to the image of Jesus Christ."

Neil Anderson, author of *Search for Significance*, speaks of how Houdini could unlock the door of any cell in which he had been placed. He was famous for it. But one time Houdini was put in a cell, and he worked on the lock for three hours and could not open it. Finally, he gave up in frustration, sat down, leaned against the door, and it swung open; it was unlocked the whole time. Sometimes, as we draw close to the exit, those around us call us crazy and run away. They just can't see that it is possible to walk through the exit and experience freedom. God gave Peter the experiences he had ("all things") so that he could become strong and one upon whom the Father could build His Church. Then Jesus instructed him, "Peter, after your conversion, strengthen your brothers." *Our brothers need to be strengthened!* This speaks of community and relationships and is the post-foundational purpose of our conversion—walking others out of the trap!

The Reward

> *[11] Thus there will be richly and abundantly provided for you **entry into the eternal kingdom** of our Lord and Savior Jesus Christ (2 Peter 1:11 AMP).*

Isn't it interesting how there are Seven Giants, seven DNA characteristics, and seven things that will give us a welcome entrance into the Kingdom? The Kingdom is supernaturally relational, so absorbing God's seven DNA the way Peter described it is actively embracing faith and moving toward *Agape*.

It is possible for us to be more comfortable in corruption than in purity because when we get to the exit, we may actually be required to take it! And many of us do not *really* want to exit. As long as we're a part of the crowd, our comfort level is high. When those around us step away, it is a different story. But the reward of walking through the trap is worth it: *a rich welcome and an abundant entrance into the eternal Kingdom.*

For years I both struggled with and was delighted by Colossians 2:6, "As you receive Christ by grace through faith, so continue to live in Him." What opened the door for me was the realization that I have already received sanctification; maturity and character come *by grace through faith.* Any good evangelical would agree that when we receive Christ and embrace the redemptive act, we have effectively entered Father's family (see John 1:12). But from that point onward our Christian culture seems to focus on doing the things that we think would make God happy. Evangelicals emphasize that we are covered with Christ's imputed righteousness and that this righteousness is progressively grafted into us. His righteousness consists of partaking of the divine nature, i.e., Christ becoming our very DNA. We no longer live because we have been displaced and Christ lives in us. We are a new creation. Why do some evangelicals never seem to grow up? Probably because they have been taught to consider themselves covered with Christ's righteousness, consequently do not see the necessity to mature. This mindset disallows us to even see the trap, let alone find the exit. It is true that we are complete in Christ, but the Kingdom process is that His own glory and virtue be imparted to us as *our very DNA*. It is about what Christ has done *for me—the redemptive act,* in order to accomplish that which He intends to accomplish *in me—Father's eternal Kingdom purpose.* This is the reward given to Father-pleasers.

The trap, the escape, and the reward are not just a new teaching. *They are a whole new way of living.* When we begin saying, "Father, I want You to lead me and guide me until there is no conflict between Your will and my own," we are emulating Jesus whose only motive was to do the Father's pleasure. Father's pleasure waits for us as we enter this Kingdom dimension. When we live by faith we are no longer trying to *be* Father-pleasers—we *are* Father-pleasers.

Freedom Is a Choice

We have been given a human will and the freedom to make choices. The Kingdom is always an offer and is never imposed, which is why salvation can get us to Heaven but is inadequate to facilitate our entrance into the Kingdom (see Acts 14:22). In the book of John, the word *Father* is used more than the word *Jesus.* Jesus wanted to give us His Father, and Father wants us to have eternal life. Thinking that eternal life is existence without time limits is nothing less than semantically raping the meaning of the word.

And this is eternal life: [it means] to know (to perceive, recognize, become acquainted with, and understand) [EQ] You, the only true and real God, and [likewise] to know Him, Jesus [as the] Christ (the Anointed One, the Messiah), Whom You have sent (John 17:3).

We tend to teach that following Christ imposes on the human will: "If you do that, you're going to hell." But the implications of *choosing* to follow Him means we will not walk in darkness. The choice is ours. Father does not say "I won't let you go with that crowd" as that would be involuntary displacement or coercion, of which *Agape* is not capable. Once righteousness is imputed it belongs to us and produces fruit. Just as carrot seeds produce carrots, Christ's Seed produces Christ. If Christ is formed in us, *we will demonstrate Christ's nature*. How do we know whether a man or woman is walking with the Lord? Jesus said we would know them by their fruits, because good, sweet, nutritious fruit cannot be imitated or humanly created. We either have it, or we do not!

When Jesus said He will take away the Kingdom and give it to those who bear fruit (see Matt. 21:43), He was referring to our inheritance. When we misrepresent the government that we claim to be serving, He withdraws our ambassadorship or the *freedom* to represent the Kingdom that we believe in. The Kingdom is then taken away from us and given to another. This is *not* talking about our eternal salvation. Christ intentionally and completely introduced personal security to His redemptive act. Bare and basic salvation is a pure gift without works or personal response for that matter.

The fruit of the Kingdom is a total different matter. Fruit is produced by the presence of or absence of God's seven attributes—His DNA. Sanctification is the same as justification and righteousness has been imputed rather than attained. Imputed means we are living under the benefits that Christ has accomplished for us; we had nothing to do with it. Imparted means Christ is being formed in me, by means of the cultivation, nourishment, and protection of that Eternal Seed received at the New Birth. Peter speaks about this with great clarity:

> *22 Since by your obedience to the Truth through the [Holy] Spirit you have purified your hearts for the sincere affection of the brethren, [see that you] love one another fervently from a pure heart. 23 You have been regenerated (born again), not from a mortal origin (seed, sperm), but from one that is immortal by the ever living and lasting Word of God (1 Peter 1:22-23 AMP).*

When the sheet was lowered the third time, Peter *yielded* to it, and only then was he *free* enough to go to Cornelius' house. I grieve over the fact that the Lord has had to bring issues to my attention three times or more before I had the capacity to embrace them! And He is doing that with me right now in some areas. Rebellion, as He told us in the Old Testament, is like witchcraft and stubbornness as idolatry. I think stubbornness is probably more offensive to God because it signifies our refusal to respond to His love.

Paul cautioned and instructed us *not* to allow our freedom to be used in a *detrimental* manner (see Gal. 5:13; 1 Pet. 2:16). The sheep and goats of Matthew 25 are revealed not as spiritually mature or not fully embracing Father's seven DNA but as acting in a corrupt and humanistic manner. Not embracing His DNA results in near or complete loss of human response leaving us dead in trespasses and sins—less human, moving toward becoming de-humanized and demonstrating animal-like behavior of biting and devouring. Religion does strange things to people.

I've counseled many people who are seeking answers, looking for the exit but only finding false doors, ones that do not lead to freedom but often to increased bondage. The deception is that the exit doesn't *look like* the correct route to freedom. And in our human reasoning, if it doesn't *look* free, then we won't *act* free, so we choose to stay in the trap.

We have to decide whether or not we are going to embrace what Father has asked. We often say to the Lord, "I believe You can part the Red Sea, but I don't believe you can deal with my anger." Or, in belief, we could say, "I believe You opened the Red Sea and I believe You have made provision for my anger, and I'm asking You to do whatever it takes and at any cost to help me exit." Believing what He says is the first step in exiting the trap. Which will you choose?

Although we know that God is *Agape*, our personal crusade, doctrine, or emphasis prevents us from yielding and giving Him a proper response. We say things like, "I forgive you, but…." It involves failure to engage and abide in the revelation of Father's nature! When we refuse to forgive due to resentments or personal "buts," we cause Father's own forgiveness to be withheld from us. Father can and does forgive us 70 times 7, but He cannot and will not cease to move us toward freedom. We need Father's mentoring process in Hebrews 12 to bring us to this freedom. It is entirely possible that any recalcitrant "but" has the capacity or strength to hold us in captivity to the prison of an *Eros* foundation. We are then ruled in sovereignty and are missing the joy and freedom of being ruled in providence. God's *providence* is our inheritance!

We need to examine our religious "but" because it is a choice—our personal preference or internal limitation. "But" means we are not able to go there and is the ultimate issue, demanding ultimate control. "But" opens us to manipulation and therefore, is as fully capable of causing the loss of our Kingdom *inheritance*, which is freely and joyfully participating with God the Father in His eternal purpose in the earth (see Rom. 8:17-21). *It is our commitment to our own preference that refuses to allow us to find the exit!* My experience suggests that when I begin to express my "but," my attitude changes, my voice changes, the climate changes, and safety and security leave the room! I know that firsthand!

I've tried to take the exit numerous times in my life, but I couldn't make the transition. When I asked the Lord why John the Baptist had to have his head removed, His response was that John simply could not make the transition from the old covenant to the new. John only knew the Old Testament God and expected Him to come and burn the chaff. Jesus came drinking wine and kissing babies! John's tribal and cultural identity would not allow him to make the transition, and he became a detriment. It is interesting that Paul, who was as deeply entrenched in the religious system as John the Baptist, through many trials and tribulations was able to make the transition. Saul's journey to becoming Paul was turbulent, spending some fourteen years in the desert while everything he ever held firm was transformed around him. His foundations were truly shaken. If we become a hindrance to Father's Kingdom, God will release us from our inheritance of being ambassadors of His government in the earth. Again, our freedom is cosmic—it contributes to the release of creation.

Mentor, Baptize and Teach

> *[18]And Jesus came up and spoke to them, saying, "All authority has been given to Me in heaven and on earth. [19]Go therefore and **make disciples** of all the nations, **baptizing** them in the name of the Father and the Son and the Holy Spirit, [20]**teaching** them to observe all that I commanded you; and lo, I am with you always, even to the end of the age" (Matthew 28:18–20).*

There are three principles of Kingdom growth that are *inexorable*: disciple/mentor; *then* baptize; *then* teach them all that I have taught you. Christ modeled these principles with His own disciples. Failing or refusing to enter the Kingdom sphere by means of mentor/baptize/ teach (see Acts 14:21-22) results in being swept up in a numbers game. Unfortunately, most churches focus on growing numbers and go around giving birth to babies by the thousands, but those who have "accepted Christ" have no one to care for, let alone mentor them. Such an evangelistic approach is now being proven to be some 180 degrees off from the clear biblical instructions given by Christ. This form of spiritual growth demonstrates numerical *obesity* rather than biblical evangelism and has no function or Kingdom purpose.

It is possible that this form of numerical growth may essentially be *cancerous,* creating in the Body of Christ something analogous to an auto-immune reaction like Lou Gehrig's disease causing the healthy body to waste away for no known reason. Growth in numbers without mentoring and teaching could also be seen as *tumorous* and consequently, malignant.

Growth that occurs abnormally has the ability to destroy that which is healthy. Like the story in Matthew 13:47-50 about the "Parable of the Net," a dragnet catches all kinds of sea life, some of which have no Kingdom value or purpose and *must be returned to the sea!* If we take in more members than we are able to mentor with biblical and Kingdom values, the entity itself becomes overwhelmed. The end result is that we are governed by the new members and have lost the governmental values and primary reasons for evangelizing in the first place. The early church's struggle to mentor and absorb some 3000 new converts demonstrates the nature of the problem.

Is it possible that *mentor/baptize/teach* is Father's answer to set the entire creation free? Mentoring in an *Agape* paradigm is designed to expose, plow up, and transform deeply held presuppositions. Both Peter and Paul were captured by the ruling religious systems of their day. In baptism we are asking for the power of those systems to be broken. Jesus said, "Why do you call Me "Lord" when other forces are actually ruling your life?" He wants to teach us how to be human as God intended. It is the reconstituting of our human personality into the image of Christ that is the salt and light in the earth. If that is lost, we are destined to be cast out into the waste pile. Evangelicalism as presently practiced has not only the capacity but the propensity to destroy and pollute the Body of Christ—the very entity that should proclaim the Kingdom and set creation free.

If we have been effectively mentored into the Kingdom and *the old creation buried in water, an effective Kingdom ambassador emerges* to teach us all that Christ and His Father wants us to know about *Agape* and the Kingdom. Colossians 1:12-13 states this clearly:

> [12]*Giving thanks to the Father, who has qualified us to share in the inheritance of the saints in Light.* [13]*For He rescued us from the domain of darkness, and transferred us to the kingdom of His beloved Son,* [14]*in whom we have redemption, the forgiveness of sins.*

As we are discipled or mentored into *Agape*, we become Father's own inheritance (see Eph. 1:18). Father-pleaser's cease reaching for their own inheritance but live to provide Father *His* inheritance—free men and women transformed by *Agape*. This helps us understand Paul's statement, *"you were called to freedom"* (Gal. 5:13). Being called to freedom means we begin to function as a governmental agent not as an ecclesiastical hireling. When we are called to freedom, it is the Kingdom mandate to be *in the world* yet not ruled by that world system, which is fully intent to govern us or impose upon us its twisted value system.

God loves the world system (see John 3:16) even though the system is caught in the five other ruling forces or arches: natural family, culture/tradition, political entities, economic entities, and religious entities. When ruled by anything other than the Kingdom we are not free to love and worship Him as He designed and intended. When we are instructed in the Kingdom we know what spirit we are of so that we can proclaim the light rather than fight the darkness. The Kingdom ambassador needs to be discipled in both the possibility and probability that we have the capacity to use or misuse our freedom.

The intended end result (*telios*) of the New Birth is *reconstituting* the human personality in the image of God, best epitomized by the Son of God becoming the Son of Man. We are regenerated through the New Birth so that we can become human as God intended—free, spontaneous, and risky and governed by *Agape*. We are here to serve the system; however, that system must not and cannot rule us.

There is no evangelism in the Great Commission; He told us to go and make disciples. Part of mentoring is the capacity and wisdom to help walk others out of bondage (the trap) and into freedom. When we do, they will be prompted to get baptized, change governments, and live in a new way. Then, we are to teach them to observe all that Father has commanded us. Such a process would cure the *obesity* problem; within 10 years, the obese Body of Christ would become healthy and fruit bearing.

I learned how mentoring is done in a practical sense from our son, Eric, and the children he adopted into Father's House in Uganda. He would bring raw, heathen children from refugee camps in Sudan into the home but never tried to *evangelize* them. He simply loved them, taught them, and trusted God to initiate in them the proper response. This process is not clean and perfect—it is messy and difficult. But after being consistently and unconditionally loved, the effects of mentoring on these children would begin to emerge. Without demand or request, they would eventually say, "Dad, I would like to live like this, and I want to be baptized."

Unfortunately, the Church has changed baptism to mean evangelism in order to get people to Heaven. We put pressure on people to believe by saying things like, "What if you hit a telephone pole on your way home and spend the rest of eternity in hell?" thinking this will motivate them to accept Christ. We use American success ethics and sales tactics to sell the "Jesus" product like we sell aluminum siding instead of discipling others until they are awakened and decide, "That's how I want to live." Many of us suffer from guilt from our earlier upbringing that we haven't presented Jesus enough. We are still in detox and need to be set free.

The entrance to this new lifestyle is water baptism, a *mentoring* subject we will address in this writing. Mentoring people to live in freedom begins with seeing that there is an alternate government. Once they have entered that Kingdom through water baptism, we then begin to teach them *everything we know*.

The Birth of Kings and Priests

> *And you shall be to Me a kingdom of priests and a holy nation. These are the words that you shall speak to the sons of Israel (Exodus 19:6).*

> *But as many as received Him, to them He gave the right to become children of God, even to those who believe in His name (John 1:12).*

> *and He has made us to be a kingdom, priests to His God and Father—to Him be the glory and the dominion forever and ever. Amen (Revelation 1:6).*

John 1:12 is an invitation into *providence* and Fatherhood. We receive a "welcome home" as we recognize the sovereign activity of God on our behalf. Our reception of that providence makes us part of His family. It then becomes our responsibility as the family of God and His own peculiar people to be His kings and priests!

In the Old Testament, Israel was a kingdom of priests and Moses led the congregation with the purpose of informing the uninformed nations of the earth about God. In the New Testament, Jesus was appointed heir of all things (see Heb. 1:2), and the Kingdom *inheritance* was taken from Moses and given to us to bring forth fruit, and Jesus now leads this congregation (see Matt.21:43). The end result is that we become His kings and priests—His inheritance—with the commission to disciple, baptize, and teach the uninformed nations and help them get out of the trap. As Father's kings and priests, we are called to instruct the nations who do not know God or the ways of God. This is the nature of mentoring. We are chosen *ambassadors* to communicate Father's reputation. David states our commission succinctly: "Give me a job teaching rebels your ways so the lost can find their way home" (Ps. 51:13 MSG). This is how we are to preach the Kingdom.

Not only have we lost the identity of the trap and recognition that we are in it, but we have also lost the exit and are failing to discover the reward Father has for us. Instead of acting as priests and offering the hurting world assistance in finding the exit, we offer them repeated forgiveness. Peter ties together our role as priests in helping others find the exit:

"Since you have in obedience to the truth purified your souls for a sincere love of the brethren, fervently love one another from the heart, for you have been born again [set in the context of the New Birth] not of seed which is perishable but imperishable [Eternal Seed], *that is, through the living and enduring word of God. For, "ALL FLESH IS LIKE GRASS, AND ALL ITS GLORY LIKE THE FLOWER OF GRASS. THE GRASS WITHERS, AND THE FLOWER FALLS OFF, BUT THE WORD OF THE LORD ENDURES FOREVER." And this is the word which was preached to you." "Therefore, putting aside all malice and all deceit and hypocrisy and envy and all slander, like newborn babies, long for the pure milk of the word, so that by it you may grow in respect to salvation, if you have tasted the kindness of the Lord. And coming to Him as to a living stone which has been rejected by men, but is choice and precious in the sight of God, you also, as living stones, are being built up as a spiritual house for a **holy priesthood*** [God is restoring His eternal purpose to instruct the nations], *to offer up spiritual sacrifices acceptable to God through Jesus Christ* (1 Peter 1:22-2:5).

God is calling for kings and priests to represent His government. Peter sees it more clearly than anyone else when he says, "But you are A CHOSEN RACE, A royal PRIESTHOOD, A HOLY NATION, A PEOPLE FOR God's OWN POSSESSION, so that you may proclaim the excellences of Him who has called you out of darkness into His marvelous light" (1 Pet. 2:9). This is a priest living in providence. Everything belongs to God. He is the Savior of all men, especially those who believe because when we ask for a heart relationship with Him, He reveals Himself providentially. He states this clearly in 1 Peter 2:10: *"For you once were NOT A PEOPLE, but now you are THE PEOPLE OF GOD; you had NOT RECEIVED MERCY, but now you have RECEIVED MERCY."*

Being a king and priest is our calling. We've trivialized calling as leading worship or playing a guitar or teaching our children in youth ministry while our true calling is to be kings and priests—what a sense of purpose that empowers us with! Being kings and priests affects every area of our life; we have purpose because we know we're representing something greater than ourselves. Suddenly what comes out of our mouths is important.

After spending seven weeks in South America I finally landed in the US. Weary and tired, I waited at baggage claim for my bags. All the suitcases came down but mine. I said to Father, "Can't You even watch over my suitcases, Lord?!" in an arrogant, smart-aleck voice. The Lord said, *"Would you like Me to give your calling to someone else?"* I knelt down at the conveyer belt and said, "If You will forgive me for my attitude, those words will never come out of my mouth again." A few minutes later my bags dropped down the conveyer belt. I think I came really close to losing my inheritance that day. This incident put the fear of God in me for the rest of my life.

So often our lives seem futile. We struggle with a sense of purpose or usefulness. I think of the widow who feels she is not needed or the retired executive who feels he has nothing to live for anymore. But they, too, are called to be kings and priests, designed to instruct other nations—those in their own circle of influence— on how God conducts His family. Did Israel do that? No. Did the early Church do that? No. Father said, "I will build My church and the gates of Hades will not overpower it" (Matt. 16:18). We are called to declare God's purpose in the earth.

So if we are kings and priests what does it mean to lose our inheritance? It does *not* mean we are going to hell. It means we are conducting ourselves in such a way that we are not properly representing the government that we claim to represent. If you are my daughter and are out running around doing everything possible that is wrong, you are still my daughter. If I am taken as a Vietnamese prisoner for ten years, I would still be an American. If we send ambassador to Greece and he becomes sexually promiscuous, misrepresents his government, or begins takings bribes, we don't take his citizenship away or electrocute him, we *relieve* him of the privilege of representing this government.

"For many are called but few are chosen" is not about our salvation but our *calling* as kings and priests. Likewise, Jesus is discussing our salvation when He says, "But small is the gate and narrow the road that leads to life, and only a few find it" (Matt. 7:14). It's the same in Revelation 2, where God gave instructions to the church at Ephesus about "removal of the lampstand." This is not about the Ephesians losing their salvation but *about their commission being removed!* Paul speaks of this as well:

> *Or do you not know that the unrighteous*
> *will not inherit the kingdom of God? Do*
> *not be deceived; neither fornicators, nor*
> *idolaters, nor adulterers, nor effeminate, nor*
> *homosexuals, nor thieves, nor the covetous,*
> *nor drunkards, nor revilers, nor swindlers,*
> *will inherit the kingdom of God* (1 Cor.
> 6:9–10).

Paul addresses similar activities including jealousies, anger, selfishness, envy, and murder that endanger our Kingdom commission in *Galatians 5:19–21*. These deeds of the flesh are the trap, and the unrighteous simply will not be allowed represent the Kingdom. They will not *inherit* the governmental purpose that was taken from Israel and given to Christ's congregation. He also said in Galatians 1:4, "Who gave Himself for our sins so that He might rescue us [the exit] from this present evil age." *This present evil age is now, our generation, not a millennium or Heaven setting.* God wants us free in *this* generation because as free kings and priests we will help set His creation free! When we get to Heaven it is all over, we won't need to be set free or set others free. The only way to escape the trap is *Agape*: "But the fruit of the Spirit is love, joy, peace, patience, kindness, goodness, faithfulness, gentleness, self-control; against such things there is no law" (see Gal. 5:22–23).

Each of us needs to ask ourselves, "Are we comfortable in the trap or are we trying to find our way out?" Father's discipline is to be a pivotal moment to allow us to continue as his kings and priests. We do not want to be comfortable in the darkness; we want to find our way out.

Peter said we are called to be kings and priests— men and women who are thoroughly oriented and familiar with the Throne. Matthew 5, 6, and 7 is the preamble to the Kingdom government[2]. The whole purpose of these chapters is to mature us emotionally and orient us to the Throne so that we can understand how God wants us to function as kings and priests.

---

[2]For more on this subject of the Kingdom government and its Constitution and Bylaws, read *The King & You* available through Lifechangers, Amazon, or Barnes & Noble

Nicodemus and the New Birth

The story of Nicodemus, found in John 3:1-21, is the clearest understanding of the New Birth or water baptism. In Nicodemus' time, many believed in Jesus and observed the signs and wonders He was performing. But Jesus was not entrusting Himself to them because He knew that all men were not maturing and properly representing the Father. They didn't follow Him because of Him; they followed Him because of the bread—they were after something. Even though most believers come for the wrong reason, the Lord still receives them. Then along came Nicodemus. He was different. Here was a man who really was trying to find his way out of the death trap. He came to Jesus by night because he would have lost his office if he had come in the daylight. Nicodemus said to Him,

> *"Rabbi, we know that you have come from God and that You are a teacher and no one can do these signs that you do unless God is with him." Jesus answered and said to him, "Truly, truly I say to you, unless you are born from above, he cannot see the Kingdom of God"* (John 3:2-3).

Nicodemus was a covenant man, a Hebrew with no concept of an eternal hell, but he knew who Christ was. He knew that the prophets of Israel said that God's people had become dry ground. He understood that this was a King and Priest fulfilling what Israel had lost because he saw Jesus doing Kingdom activity (healing people, ministering to them, preaching the Kingdom), and he experienced *awakening*. Because of this he asked if the Kingdom was being restored. He and everyone in that day were anticipating the Messiah coming to get rid of the Romans, and he wanted to help.

There is nothing mentioned in the Old Testament about life after death except the mention of *Sheol*, the land of the dead. So, when Jesus said, "Very truly I tell you, no one can see the kingdom of God unless they are born again," Nicodemus couldn't quite figure out what Jesus was saying. He asked, "How one can be born again when he is old?" (vs. 4) and exclaimed, "He cannot enter a second time into his mother's womb and be born, can he?" Nicodemus was asking for a providential call to Kingdom purpose. He was told he must be born from above not so it could be determined whether or not he went to Heaven or hell but so he could find his way out of the trap and into the Kingdom. Jesus' response to Nicodemus was, "Truly, truly, I say to you, unless one is born of water and the Spirit he cannot *enter* into the kingdom of God" (John 3:5). Jesus told Nicodemus that he must first be able to *see* so that he could enter.

We enter the Kingdom dimension by baptism and resurrection into a new creation—that sphere where Father's will and pleasure are the governing force. Seeing is one thing, entering is another, and that does not happen in some simultaneous event when we come to Christ. It happens progressively. The New Birth is the result of our opening to Father and saying, "I want You to rule over me; I am asking for Your providential governing purpose in my daily life." This gives us the ability to *see* another sphere that can only be seen and entered into by those who have given God the freedom to govern them by means of the person of Christ (see Acts 14:22). We receive freedom from the *Eros* in ourselves as well as from all five world systems. Kingdom freedom includes freedom from the law, from fear, and from the idea of human works. We establish a foundation governed by *Agape* DNA living as Father-pleasers, measuring success or failure by means of an *Agape* filter.

How then does Christ come into this? Following our reception of Christ and the insemination of *Agape* as the eternal, uncreated and incorruptible Seed, Christ utilizes water baptism by burial of the old creation, i.e., the waters of Noah (see Isa. 54:9 in context) burying us to all the corruption of that old creation and leading us to the exit, which is Himself, and to the freedom He promised. If we can properly understand our New Birth, we can also re-interpret over one hundred years of inadequate teaching. It is not about salvation, understood as repeated forgiveness, but about entering that realm identified as the Kingdom of God. It is a sphere where Father's will is known and embraced. It is not a location but a relational reality.

What does it mean to be reborn? It involves a change of governments—moving from one of the arche of the world systems (natural family, culture/tradition, political entities, economic entities, religious entities) to Kingdom reality. An arche or principality forms when it intentionally or unconsciously strays from its created purpose, intention, or assignment. The essence of the transition is moving from an entity to a system.[3] Father uses the analogy of water to symbolize death to all five arches and the burying this world's systems. Thus, baptism is referred to as "the waters of Noah" or burial of the corruption of the world system. When we are reborn, a new man emerges. It includes so much more than being forgiven. When we give birth to our children, a new *person* emerges out of the womb, and Jesus was saying that in the New Birth we are no longer going to do things the way we did it before. We are going to receive an Eternal Seed of God's DNA in Christ that contains the capacity and energy to produce what Father wants. When we receive that Eternal Seed, a birth is inexorably scheduled to take place although the actual birthing into the Kingdom dimension is multi-faceted. He saved us (past tense). He is saving us (present tense). He will save us (future tense). For us to be offered *forgiveness* without the intended Kingdom dimension is to have been given half the story. Nicodemus wanted a new government, but Jesus

[3]For more information on this important subject, read *Dr. Frankenstein and World Systems* available through Lifechangers, Amazon, or Barnes & Noble.

responded that the government of God comes through the New Birth. To our knowledge, Nicodemus never gave evidence that he had fully embraced being born from above but he did appear again at the tomb. Like many others, Nicodemus discovered himself in some kind of process, seeking to understand the nature and implications of this new governmental Kingdom.

We have been teaching that "*enter the Kingdom*" is limited to being defined by our destiny being changed from hell to Heaven. The Kingdom is *not* Heaven. Matthew uses the phrase *Kingdom of heaven* (see Matt. 5:20; 7:21; 18:3) and the other Gospels use the phrase *Kingdom of God* (see Mark 9:47; 10:23; Luke 18:24-25) because the Hebrew caution refused to state God's name for fear of using it wrongly. For example, when I say, "Heaven bless you," I'm saying, "God bless you" without using the word *God*. But Jesus used the phrase *Kingdom of God* everywhere except in Matthew.

In Malachi, the glory departed and was received into Heaven. For 430 years there was no sound from Heaven. Everything seemed dead or dying. Suddenly, John the Baptist appears on the scene, assigned to prepare a way for Jesus. Jesus appears teaching about a birth from above because the New Jerusalem, the source of governmental authority is from above. The old Jerusalem no longer has anything to offer. No wonder Nicodemus was stunned. His encounter with this Kingdom was a progression of courage. He had to show up, ask hard questions, and confront the difficult answers. Nicodemus was looking for a restoration of the anointing and promise of his King and Priest.

The Role of Kings and Priests

The role of kings and priests is to properly represent Father and help others see the exit out of the trap. The act and function of a priest can be stated by this acronym: A.L.I.V.E.

Absorb human failure. Jesus did it so we are called to do it. I think one of the hardest things to do is to see human failure and not try and correct it. Correcting failure and absorbing failure are two different things.

Love without reward. Unfortunately our churches tend to struggle with this one, especially in intercessory prayer groups. We tend to forget the confidentiality piece that needs to be present. Many intercessory groups I've seen as a pastor are a viper's nest. We say, "I just want you to know about this so we can pray together." Mercy! A friend of mine drove 50 miles to talk to his pastor about an emotional feeling he had for another woman. There was no transgression, just an attraction. The pastor told his wife, and she called her friend who knew my friend's wife, and before he got home, his wife knew about it. It traumatized their marriage, and all he was trying to do was get some help. We need to learn how to love each other without any reward, even simply being "in the know."

Vocational suffering. There are some things we will suffer just because we are kings and priests. There won't seem to be any reason for the suffering, no sin or failure. Vocational suffering is just part of our training and journey.

Extender of mercy. Often when we think of being a Priest and King we think of ruling, not extending mercy. The king has authority to rule, and the priest has a mediatory role. But it is a symbiosis. We function in both and exercise authority in both, but we are to do so in a priestly way. When we exercise our authority, it doesn't come out like the Gentiles exercising control and tyranny over others. If we exercise our *fatherhood* with our family in anything less than a priestly way our family will not respond to our authority.

Nicodemus recognized that he had lost his inheritance and needed Jesus to show him how to get it back. Jesus told him the only way to get it back was through a rebirth. *Can we see that this New Birth is the exit?!* It seems that most of us go thru a breach birth, where we are only partially reborn, getting stuck in the birth canal.

Unless we are emotionally mature and find the exit to the trap, we will do exactly what Israel did with its' own Kingdom inheritance: distort, fail, abuse, or reject it. Paul, in Romans 11:26, tells us that "all Israel will be saved." But Father withdrew His governmental commission from Israel until the purpose could be fulfilled by both Jew and Gentile. There was a need for

One New Man. Because this *ambassadorship* is Kingly and Priestly, we want to properly represent Him. But in doing so we cannot play emotional or financial games with this calling. We are to instruct the uninformed nations, and that is why we disciple, baptize, and teach. Our New Birth produces this new man. If a new man is not being born, then the process is flawed, breached, or aborted. Some degree of insight will be required to identify and agree that this is, indeed, the circumstantial condition that prevails in the west.

To review, our governmental purpose is not limited to Heaven or hell; we are called to be kings and priests. We can either set creation free or add to its contamination and failure. This should give us such an awesome sense of purpose and reason for being! We are here to set creation free! Personal salvation is removed from its false center, allowing the Kingdom center to function as the biblically assigned center.

Agape: The Exit from the Trap

The exit from the trap is supernatural. Sometimes it is difficult to talk about the supernatural with present-day adults. It's like telling a three-year olds' fairy tale to a cynical, intelligent adult and expecting him to fall for it. Just telling people who are running from the exit that there's a supernatural way out is not going to work. We have to encourage them to begin to perceive truth and ask God to reveal it to them. Seeing the exit from the trap is a moment of *illumination of us actually being in the trap*. We cannot see the exit until we understand that we, personally, are imprisoned. But, understanding that we are in the trap does not automatically mean we are free or willing to choose the exit. We don't get a free, one-time "Get Out Of Jail" card. What happens is the Lord increases our understanding of the nature of the trap. It would be great if we could just pray the prayer of salvation and find Jesus, but that is not the answer. The trap itself is progressive bondage, in a similar manner getting free is progressive. We all have people in our lives that are paralyzed because they are so pickled in the trap, yet they may or may not be begging for help to get out. We teach others about the exit by demonstrating and proclaiming the Kingdom of *Agape*. It is a progressive, organic unfolding of the Father's DNA day-by-day, decision-by-decision. We encourage them to get up, walk out, and live out the growth, development, and emergence of the Father's DNA and character of Christ formed in us.

Agape is reformational. We are at the same crossroads as Jesus. It may be that we are close to what He was saying to those other villages when He said, "*Repent, the Kingdom of God is at hand.*" Does this mean we may be required to change what it means to preach Christ? Absolutely! Embracing His DNA makes us one with Him. The Lord seems to offer us some kind of intimate, grand entrance into an eternal Kingdom. It is Christ in us that is this the hope of glory, which is synonymous with the Kingdom. If we embrace His DNA and allow Father to re-center us, it releases us into freedom and an enriched welcome in the Kingdom (see 2 Pet.1:11). And the Kingdom results in righteousness, peace, and joy because it is *in the Holy Spirit*! Only a person who is free can enjoy righteousness, peace, and joy.

There is nothing above *Agape* because God is *Agape*. There is no place you can go above *Agape* because that is His nature, and that is where we are heading. It is not ironic that Peter ended with *Agape*. It is *Agape* that takes the strain and pressure out of relationships because we can hear the Father more clearly and respond to Him more gently.

But thou art making me, I thank thee, sire.
What thou hast done and doest thou know'st well,
And I will help thee: gently in thy fire
I will lie burning; on thy potter's-wheel
I will whirl patient, though my brain should reel.
Thy grace shall be enough the grief to quell,
And growing strength perfect through weakness dire.
George MacDonald
Diary Of An Old Soul, October 2

Suggested Reading

Transforming Mission by David Bosch
Pathological Altruism by Barbara Oxley

About the Author

Bob Mumford is a dynamic Bible teacher with a unique and powerful gift for imparting the Word of God. His anointed messages are remembered years afterwards because he captivates his audiences by humor in the form of word pictures, which penetrate deep into hearts with incredible authority, clarity, and personal application. Since 1954, thousands of Christians worldwide have attributed their spiritual growth and determination to follow Jesus Christ to his prophetic teaching, helping them understand Father God and His Kingdom.

Bob has written for major Christian periodicals both in the United States and abroad and published several books including *The Agape Road, The Mysterious Seed, Nourishing the Seed, Take Another Look at Guidance, The King & You, Fifteen Steps Out, The Purpose of Temptation, and Journey to the Father.* He has also published numerous booklets called *Plumblines*, including *Renegade Male* and a series on *Inheritance*. Bob's writings have been translated into many different languages.

Bob has a heart for backsliders, having come to the Lord at age 12 only to stray from God a few months later. After being away from God for 12 years, the Lord cleaned up his heart and gave him new purpose and direction, calling him specifically to "Feed My Sheep."

After completing his High School education in the Navy and then graduating with a Bachelor of Science in Bible from Valley Forge Christian College, Bob Mumford attended the University of Delaware and then received his Masters of Divinity degree from Reformed Episcopal Seminary in Philadelphia. Over the years, he has served as a pastor and as Dean and Professor of New Testament and Missions at Elim Bible Institute. In 1972, he founded Lifechangers, Inc. to distribute his teaching materials all over the world where he has traveled extensively to some 50 nations as an international conference speaker.

Today he is considered to be a spiritual "Papa" to thousands of Christians. His ministry has been to prophetically proclaim and teach the sufficiency of Christ Jesus and His Kingdom in a manner which promotes reconciliation and unity in the Body of Christ. Bob seeks to bring about personal spiritual change and growth in the life of every believer, regardless of denominational persuasion.

Bob and his wife, Judith, reside in Raleigh, North Carolina where they are surrounded by their children and grandchildren. If you would like to receive information on Bob Mumford's ministry Lifechangers, you can contact us at:

LIFECHANGERS

P.O. Box 3709, Cookeville, TN 38502 U.S.A.
www.lifechangers.org / lc@lifechangers.org
931.520.3730 / 800.521.5676

Other Titles by Bob Mumford

Books
The *Agape* Road
The Mysterious Seed
Nourishing the Seed
Fifteen Steps Out
Take Another Look at Guidance
The King & You
The Purpose of Temptation
Dr. Frankenstein & World Systems

Bible Studies
The *Agape* Road
Breaking Out (only in Spanish)
Knowing, Loving & Following Jesus
Unshared Love

Booklets
Acting Against Myself
Becoming a Father Pleaser
Being Bilingual
Below the Bottom Line
Burnt Stones
Church of My Dreams
Correction Not Rejection
Difference Between the Church and Kingdom
Dr. Frankenstein & World Systems
Forever Change
Gang of Ugly Facts
Giving and Receiving Offense
God's Final Speech

Grace: God's Rubber Room
Human as God Intended
Implications of Following Jesus
Inconveniently Enlightened
Inflamed Desire
It Came to Pass
Journey to the Father
Kingdom as Father, Church as Mother
Koinonia
Laboring to Rest
Law of Flexibility
Lifting Weights in Father's Gym
On Being Scandalized
Over to You, Lord
Prison of Resentment
Psalm for Living
Renegade Male
Riddle of the Painful Earth
Sitting in Darkness, Walking in Light
Standing in the Whirlwind
Three Dimensional Reality
Transforming Human Behavior
Water Baptism
When God Changed His Address
Why God?

These books and many others are available through Lifechangers.

www.ingramcontent.com/pod-product-compliance
Lightning Source LLC
Chambersburg PA
CBHW071824020426
42331CB00007B/1600